Butterfly Farmer

- Jaroslav (Jerry) Petryshyn -

Poems

FriesenPress

Suite 300 - 990 Fort St
Victoria, BC, Canada, V8V 3K2
www.friesenpress.com

Copyright © 2015 by Jaroslav (Jerry) Petryshyn
First Edition — 2015

ISBN
978-1-4602-6243-6 (Hardcover)
978-1-4602-6244-3 (Paperback)
978-1-4602-6245-0 (eBook)

1. Poetry

Distributed to the trade by The Ingram Book Company

Table of Contents

Books by Jaroslav (Jerry) Petryshyn

Peasants in the Promised Land: Canada and the Ukrainians 1891–1914 (1985)

A Sense of Community: Grande Prairie Regional College 1966–91 (1991)

Made up to a Standard: Thomas Alexander Russell and
the Russell Motor Car Company (2000)

Dr. Jaroslav (Jerry) Petryshyn is an award winning author who has
written extensively on Canadian history. This is his first book of poetry.

I dedicate these poems to Diane, Alisha and Halyna
No hidden meanings – just love

Introduction

Poetry is about observation, imagination and seemingly non-sequitur connections. So it is with this collection. The poems are divided into three overlapping parts that diverge and converge at various points. The first twenty-five poems are about nature – or rather encounters that piqued my imagination in some indelible way that was both particular and universal. For the most part, these poems evolved around having evening cigars while watching earthly creatures going about their existence in the quiet of the dark. The next twenty-one poems (Part Two) explore the self with concomitant overtones to the natural world. Themes include the power of memories, growing old, vanity and eclectic matters in between. These germinated in the same still darkness at times when I was not distracted by animal behaviour. The final seven poems (Part Three), more whimsical in thought and outer worldly in subject, may appeal to younger readers. In a sense, these are residual pieces that have crept in – perhaps unconsciously – even as I was preoccupied with work on the other poems. The one exception is the *Dinosaur Song*, a nonsensical ditty (music not provided) written in a Wizard of Oz moment for my young daughters over twenty-five years ago.

These poems started out as a personal challenge. Poetry was a genre that I knew little about let alone attempt to compose. To extrapolate in a few poignant words or lines not only the narrative but the often ephemeral sense of the narrative in a nuanced and meaningful way seemed a formidable task. As I moved from nonfiction, academic historical writing to the literary stream and in the spirit of attempting the most daunting first, poetry appeared the appropriate starting point. As such, I experimented with a variety of styles and templates – from traditional rhyme and rhythm motifs to what might be called unfettered free verse.

In any case, poetry is very much like Art – a matter of personal experiences and taste. Hopefully, this work has a sufficient combination of language, structure and versatility to strike a resonance with the reader.

Part 1

The Mole and Me

Flat field – brown stubble filled.

Naked stump – cut clean.

Me sitting, corona smoke snaking white whiffs into the still sky.

A tranquil moment when the sun fades scarlet,

The darkness still closet bound.

Empty thoughts surround like silence in a church.

Lazy glance downward, a bundled blur occupied,

Strangely unperturbed by my form.

A Mole, shrouded in sparse blades of brush.

I remained transfixed, as the rodent gorged, paused, raised his head, scented the air

And satisfied, returned to his fare.

A courageous act I thought to be so exposed,

Innately aware of swooping shadows above – prey stalkers below.

Time passed in nervous calm, the Mole regularly repeating this ritualized refrain.

As the light gave out, the Mole too winked away

Back into his black abyss, safe for another day.

I simply sat and pondered his bold appearance

Until the corona burned out.

Our Max

Buddha's gift; Emperor's prize
Groomed by eunuchs of the court.
Amusing, hearth warming, playful mate
Steadfast keeper of the royal gate.
Bred to bark at urgent pitch should strangers call
Or sudden shadows cast the wall.

Our Max is of this 'little lion' stock;
A litter runt who grew not much.
And while destined to a soft bellied life
Still remains son of a Shih Tzu, purposeful and proud
Who once protected the regal realm.
These things he was and with him stayed
'Til old age and shaky limbs diluted his domain.
Now he simply sleeps in beguiled dreams.

Once he was agile and quick
A dauntless dart in the backyard chase.
Whether shaggy spooled in curled locks
Or cut less wild to short tight tufts,
Our Max partook in brilliant bursts
Yet remained reserved more often than not
Taking umbrage at suggested walks.

Perhaps early trauma forged this trait
When lost, alone to meet his fate
He survived, was found and brought back to us.
Yet fearful of further treks
Resolutely sat, front legs anchored stiff in protest

To such wanton schemes.
Now he simply sleeps in beguiled dreams.

White motes spread in each eye
His albino hollows diffuse the light
Barely penetrating his glassy gaze.
He stares at cupboard doors or grassy nodes
Into blind bursts of opaque haze.
Yet he stands tall when taken out, his matted mane
Disturbing the breeze
For it's through his cold, wet nose he views the wind.

Almost human in his numerous ills
He eats his gruel laced with pills
With deliberate care in a delicate way.
At night he lays, his body spewed
In our laps at intervals.
Quality time for him, it seems,
Is to simply sleep in beguiled dreams.

Thanks Max

Our Max died today
A good death, a planned death
On his yellow 'blanky' relaxed,
Legs stretched out leisurely,
Soft paws delicately curled,
Head tilted just so in gentle repose
Caressed by his mothership.

Our Max died today
But the memories remain alive
Indelibly enshrined in those special moments
Of pause and recollection.
Thanks Max for fourteen years of loving life
That touched us all.

'Branta Canadennis'

They came in heavy, a matrix of noise
Big breasted birds with magnificent poise
Tumultuously clacking in regal refrain
Canvassing shrewdly their new domain.
They hit earth thickly, a resounding thump
Impacting precisely like a sumo stomp.

Gaggle of geese on grain filled sod
In clumps they gathered, a disciplined flock.
While long necked ganders on the outer row
Kept nervous watch for dangerous foe.
Honks subsiding they scouted their feed
And began their scouring for scattered seed.

A week they stayed amid salubrious yield
Bingeing for hours they fallowed the field
'Til by some collective decree
They flew off in a ragged vee.
Having such fare so free to extract
There was no doubt they'd be back.
They swung around for one last lap
The place marked firmly on their map.

Battle of the Bell

Winter almost gone, spring ascending
One last bird seed bell still left hanging.
Hooked by a shoelace looped o'er an apple tree limb
Once fully shaped now nipped and gouged thin.

A flock of black – capped Chickadees seeing their chance
Arrived flitting in frenzied dance.
Behold the 'blue plate special' from which there was to pick
Savoury seeds suitably served on a serrated stick.

Focussed steadfastly on their aerial mission
They missed from below their chief competition.
A black squirrel scampered from the nearby weeds
And shrewdly surveyed those same seeds.

He hurried up the trunk to claim the prize
Catching the Chickadees in stunned surprise.
Attaching his hind claws to the bristled bark
He stretched downward into a triumphant arc.

The rodent ate ravenously until almost filled
While the Chickadees hovered and shrilled.
Not finished yet he had a thought
And swung the remnants onto the branch top.

More relaxed, he dined at a leisurely pace.
The Chickadees dispersed into time and space.
He packaged the last portions into his mouth
Vacated his perch and tail raised high, headed south.

'Bird on a Wire'

From on high a Robin reconnoitred then dropped earthbound
Spotting objects of interest on the dew drenched ground.
The dark, black head and red brick breast denoted a male,
A robust specimen with a long, straight tail.
He hopped and he bopped locating his fare
Occasionally stopping to give me a stare.
All was fine for a while until he had enough
And as I edged closer, he promptly flew off.
He swooned onto a most unlikely spot,
A clothes line that I helped to put up.
It alas developed an egregiously bad sag
Which he aggravated into a wild, warped wag.
Caught out completely by the sudden shift,
'Bird on a Wire' begot a new twist.
Wings flapping, feathers far flung, he barely straightened himself out.
Quite unbecoming – his thrashing about.
Bemused, I indulged in uncharitable thinking:
From what eavestrough has this bird been drinking?

Casualty Cleaner

Black lump, white stripe in pools of rich red:
The proverbial dead skunk in the middle of the road.
A nocturnal sojourn broke bad by a 'flatbed'.
The fresh kill barely gelled before a cleaner showed.

He arrived magically in early dawn
Dark, silvery wings, serrated tips spread across the sky.
From afar he appeared majestically drawn
Like a hawk surfing the current, soaring high.

Once he alighted the image changed.
Shrivelled, scarlet head attached to an oversized frame
Draped in a sombre onyx robe, loosely arranged.
He surveyed the entrails, then the rest of the game.

While aware of objects approaching his fare,
He remained quite placid, keeping his stride.
They would slow he seemed to know because he was there
Affording indulgence – a sample or two – before hopping aside.

Carrion eater – cum – casualty cleaner
All part of natural order and culture.
To be the funereal fowl, a repugnant reaper
Is the role of the Turkey Vulture.

The Lonesome Dove

Along our rooftop a solitary dove silhouetted the sky
Primly pacing while croo – croo wooing a mournful cry.
Each day in mid-afternoon as I lit my corona at our garage door
He'd start his ritual reciting of the same sad score.

While admittedly annoying, this incessant call of despair
Emerged unfiltered from the survivor of a bonded pair.
A cat or car, matters not how the other met her fate
Only that he was left alone croo – croo – wooing for his mate.

My empathy remained tempered by his repeated bray
That echoed epistles of distress and dismay.
Time passed, then, he 'whistled' off forever gone
Strangely, I do miss him but not his croo – croo wooing song.

Of Mice and Me

The Bic sparks against the coal black night – the corona glows.
Amid quiet brooding, I stand framing the garage doorway, peering out
When from the rafters and bins behind, ominous sounds arose.
Pitter – patter claws, scuttling scrapes and objects moved about.

It took but one carcinogenic drag to decipher.
Mice had invaded, spewing fecal fibril, forging narcissistic nests.
The reality could not be avoided – I'd have to play the 'Pied Piper'
To rid my place of these plenteous pests.

I had on hand one wooden mouse trap
That baited and set, would start my chore.
It was advertised as a 'swift kill with a snap'.
Rigged rudely with prejudice, I placed it on the floor.

The very next day I found it sprung.
The rodent lay pinned, eyes wide, the mouth in surprised O.
A hind limb had been mangled by the steel spring rung.
A swift, decent death alluded him, disturbingly so.

Lifting the bar, I took the mouse out by the tail.
Cowardly perhaps, I did not end his life fast
Instead, laid him down near a grassy trail;
Dispassionate Nature would do the rest.

Unaccountably chastened by this event, I turned suitably sublime
On a new course of action, less visceral, more detached.
A package of special blue cubes laced with strychnine
Planted strategically, ensured they'd be efficiently dispatched.

A human, if not humane, thing to do – the battle lines had been drawn.

No need to see the violence nor dispose of what remain.

They'd ingest, slink away and die somewhere calm.

And I'd smoke the corona quietly brooding in my silent domain.

Toads

Odd, I hadn't seen a toad for a long while
Nor thought about them since I was a juvenile.
Did they succumb to some ecocidal scourge
Or have they survived, resilient to any such purge?

Then, unexpectedly, I spied one against the inner garage door.
He seemed to hush the air around him and melt into the floor.
On a small plastic shovel I carried him out to a grassy node
Presuming he belonged there and would blend into the fold.

A week later, on the back porch at dusk, I almost sat
On a bloated, reddish brown blob – faint white line grooved down the back;
Squat with blotchy skin attached to sticky, knobbed feet
Calmly camped on the pine bench seat.

He was perfectly still, patiently awaiting his fare,
His long, agile tongue poised to flick and snare.
I did not disturb his silent, inert hunt
But watched the warty form without affront.

Shortly after, I took our dog Max to his preferred 'piddle' lot
And almost stepped on yet another lumpy sac
Settled squarely in the middle of Max's well marked spot.
The toad took no notice – did not move.
The dog sniffed cautiously – did not approve.
Both Max and I let him be.

Backdrop bumps; lunar rock lumps
Plain sight hiding while benignly stalking their prey
Indeed toads are surviving in their own peculiar way.

Once Upon a Possum

A moonlit possum waddled across
The dark garage doorway
As I stood lurking out
Like a shadow swallowed voyeur
Out for an evening stalk.

Double take: A possum this far north?
But there was no mistake;
What else had an extended snout,
A mousey pale face, a long string tail
Attached to a rounded, stuffed body
Moving at a plodding pace?

He didn't notice my presence
Or the curling smoke exhausted
From my cheap corona
But went about his business
Around the hedge and corner
Into the black abyss.

Compelled to record my first possum sighting
My thoughts drew blank, then eerily askew.
Images of Jed Clampett, Jethro and Elly May barged in
Complete with an iron cauldron
And Granny Clampett stirring possum stew.

When Apples Fall

When apples fall what does it matter?
A frivolous question perhaps
Best asked at High Tea with the Mad Hatter
Or other such knowing chaps.

But then I spied a squirrel out for a daily scoot.
He seized a number of apples for his secret nests.
As well, wandering Warblers eyed the fallen fruit,
Pecked on blemished burrows and swallowed the wiggly guests.

Wasps flew down in clumps to extract the nectar spill
While Lady Bugs in bunches staked out their own sweet space.
Later, two reclusive deer arrived from over a weed filled hill
And dined on those ground bound apples with gentle grace.

So my frivolous question was not that at all.
And though I'd like High Tea with the Mad Hatter,
Discuss gravity and Newton's second law,
I'd emphatically affirm that fallen apples do matter.

Butterfly Farmer

Beyond the long, lustrous lawn lay my great neglected kingdom –
Clumps of Devil's grass, entangled vines, struggling shrubs and a milkweed fiefdom:
Tall stands of broad leaves, pink – purple clusters adjoined to soft ridged, pale green pods
Noxious, 'bush hog' fodder – and yet, the elixir, butterfly flower.

From the mountains of Central Mexico carried on continental currents they come.
Temporal travellers on a three generation journey to my monarch butterfly farm.
They flit in graceful fragility in the sun warmed air like shuttlecocks caught in a breeze
Attracted to their one and only need.
What irony that these poisonous plants and crop contaminants should hold the key
To this monarchical dynasty and that they should thrive in my see.

Capricious caterpillars wrapped in yellow tinged white and black stripes suddenly appear
From beneath the milkweed's canopy.
Tiny pin heads at first, they devour their egg sheaths
Before sallying on to the red-veined leaves.
The host and hatchery thus becomes the food emporium.
Unrepentant, they gorge and grow thick then start spinning a silky mix –
Threaded pads bound to stem and branches that finally encase them completely
To hang like mummified mutants in their chrysalises
'Til emerged metamorphosed into the monarch butterfly – fourth generation.

The slender, dark bodies coalesce while the black laced, orange wings beat to harden.
Suddenly, they're free to scour the milkweed mews
Sagaciously sucking copious amounts of milky nectar,
Immune to the nourishing toxins that put predators at risk.
Replenished so, they lift aloft to ride the winds south to the Mexican mountains;
There mate and restart the cycle.
My only chore – bear witness and keep the unkempt field pure.

*   *   *

The first year I had a lovely monarch crop.

This year not so much; they just didn't show.

I was saddened – my disappointment profound.

The milkweeds, though, continued to flourish throughout their fiefdom

Abundantly spewing seed tufts to find firm root in the ground.

Maybe next year – I can farm again.

Close Encounter

Late autumn in Banff, a light layer of snow salted the ground. Don and I ascend Sulphur Mountain along a well-worn path en route to the Cosmic Ray Station at the top. "No, it's not the home of the Fantastic Four," I mused, "but a national historic park with plaques and interpretive artefacts commemorating Canada's contribution to high altitude studies in the late fifties. We'll walk around and take the gondola down." "Sounds good to me," he said. "Cosmic rays eh – from outer space ... didn't they give those comic book characters their super powers?" "Actually, Stan Lee did," I replied.

The subject was left there and I didn't give it a second thought until halfway up. Suddenly, compelled by some primal force, I vigorously whirled about – the proverbial sixth sense violently aroused. I gasped at the Elk at large who abruptly stopped her charge coming to a skidding halt about a metre from where we stood stunned. My unexpected action had broken her run.

"What the h- elk!" I exclaimed with unabashed alarm. This malevolent 'Wapiti' could do us harm! Her head was raised high, ears pinned back, nostrils flared, rivers of jagged red ran through her wide, angry eyes. But what really made us afraid was the tight, crooked mouth foaming white froth between the hisses.

"What do we do?" I said softly to my friend. "I dunno," he replied, exhibiting a calm that belied any prospects of a happy ending. Fortunately, it seemed that the copper tanned Elk with dark intentions was as stupefied as us. Awkward seconds passed – a forever tick of time. All parties remained motionless caught locked in a stare off.

Then, by innate telepathic ingestion, in unison we choreographed ourselves toward a giant pine doing our best Charlie Chaplin shuffle hoping not to ruffle the agitated animal. Once behind the tree, we grew measurably bolder, threw snowballs in her direction and yelled warnings to other trail goers.

After a further contemplative pause, the Elk appeared satisfied that we posed no overt threat. With a final percussive snort, she turned and at a leisurely pace hoofed back up the mountain face.

I don't know why the Elk became so belligerent – protecting her offspring, bad buck day at the *rut* or maybe she just didn't like our looks!

"None of the above," whispered a superhero voice from the distant reaches of my mind.

"It was those cosmic rays that made her schizo and think that you were aliens invading her domain."

With no field guide on the effects of cosmic rays on Elk, that's as good an explanation as any.

The Lone Gander

A lone gander flew overhead
Below, I wondered why.
He seemed irate and increasingly desperate
Screeching harrowing honks at intervals:
"Hey guys – where'd yah go?"
The warmth of autumn had long since past;
Days were cold and grey with the snow
Building to a crescendo –
The wind having a blast.
Probably tough winging up there
For this gadabout gander
Who dallied far too long
And missed his ride south.
Perhaps the feed was too rich;
Maybe life got too comfortable;
Or he just became lazy.
And when he wasn't looking
They flocked off.

Spoilers

A warm summer evening – the air hangs limp –
Made magic by potpourris of sweet grassy smells.
A serendipitous silence settles over the land.

Spoiled by multiple choruses of sex starved male crickets
Rubbing forewings in agitated foreplay –
Back and forth, back and forth at a frenetic pace
In an endless cacophony of caustic chirps.

I know that it's their opera house.
Still, I wish upon a star that they all get laid simultaneously
And stop those grating sounds.
Then, the night would be perfect.

The Dog Who Knew Better

Pete's Jack Russell was extreme – even for the breed.

Strung tighter than a longbow's string,

Cerk would sniff, snort and snap – chase whatever moved

Then emerge nonplussed from a nearby bush and piss on one's shoe.

An incessant yapper, he seemed possessed by distempered ticks always scratching

Or rubbing his short coarse coat against some rough edged post.

He had the attention span of a gnat – didn't obey the usual commands

'Stop' 'Heel' – let alone learn dog tricks.

Still, he wagged his tail and took to wild auto rides

Which ensured he'd go on our fishing trip.

Pete drove his Honda furiously fast with rally car racer skill

Over the potted oil rig roads west of Beaverlodge.

He grinned as he drove – "Speed gives Cerk a thrill."

Well into the foothills we reached our destination

An unnamed little lake about a half mile from where we parked

That Pete swore was used in a beer commercial –

Greenish blue, mid-summer placid where trout gave an invitation

Jumping out of the water in anticipation of our casting flies.

Exaggeration, perhaps, but occasionally fish did jump from this emerald jewel

As we set up camp on the outstretching shore.

The small tent erected, our personal gear sorted,

We laid gathered sticks on the hard rocky ground, built a fire,

Heated canned stew and topped it off with a bit of brew.

Cerk too enjoyed himself in numerous romps – got rewarded

In the dire darts of Chipmunks and other rodents.

With the late June sun sinking into the horizon

The embers smouldering and finally dying, we retired.
The dog followed, contently settling in a corner of our cozy tent.

In the wee hours of the morning a loud thump, then twap
Against the fragile fabric of our shelter, ended sleep.
"What was that?" I whispered instantly alert.
Pete roused, got his bearings, cautiously unzipped and peered out.
The dawn's early light was just an Eastern slit
But the outline was there – a large black bear fussing about the site
Rising high on his hinds toward the dangling backpack.
Pete eased toward his sleeping bag and to my surprise produced a rifle.
Popping in a shell, he ventured out, stood and fired,
The barrel pointed upward over the lake.
The boom shattered the peace and sent a shudder through the trees,
Scattering all manner of wild life through the foliage.
On the bear, though, it was less dramatic.
Instead of a hurried exit, he simply turned and stared.
We returned the same with frozen 'oh oh' on our faces.
It was about a ten second standoff before the beast decided to move on.
There wasn't much tasty in that hanging catch – probably didn't smell that sweet.

Relief was followed by a flashing thought – where's Cerk!
Hastily we searched the grounds and found
'Man's best friend' exactly where he settled down earlier in the night.
He was assuredly aware of the bear – his eyes wide and diamond sharp –
Yet, he had not budged a muscle or provided a bark,
Our 'perpetual motion' canine had suddenly become discreet
An inert statue rooted in place to an anchored tether.
I misjudged this delinquent terrier: here's a dog who knew better.
I guess he figured humans can fend for themselves against this 'beast of prey'
Best save the chase for another day.

Squirrel Speak

Two black squirrels sat on the bare branch of a massive Maple tree
Vociferously chattering, their attention riveted on a small Shih Tzu
Doing his business on the frozen snow below.
This elevated jabber tweaked my wonder and reflection.
What did these sentient squirrels convey in their excited conversation?
Feral fear? Animated annoyance? Ignoble indignation? Raucous ridicule?
Casual curiosity? Averse amusement? Or some variant in between?
Alas, with no Dr. Dolittle to decipher squirrel speak
Any speculation was moot – really quite pointless.
Pity that – they most emphatically said their piece.
Not that it mattered to our little Max, blind and hard of hearing,
Quite oblivious to the rodents' noisy natter
He sniffed a spot, raised a hind leg and had a dismissive wiz.

Squirrel Speak 'Part Deux'

Two squirrels engaged in remonstrative chatter
Parting company in noisy disagreement.
One scurried up a pole and with athletic grace
Skipped along the thick, black wire
To the opposite side of the road.
The other gave his tail a demonstrative flick
As if to say "I don't do show-off tricks".
And scooted across the asphalt
Only to be shmucked by a speeding truck
Before he reached the middle.
From above, the chatter stopped
As his traumatized companion glared at the tire track mark
With the bushy tail sticking out.
Do it my way or the highway
Took on a whole new meaning.

Elk Run Down

The Wolf Pack caught the Elk midway on the lake
After a prolonged, exhausting chase.
The legs slackened, splayed and she went for a final slide
In wide eyed terror across the snow and ice
Before she died.
A telltale trough of entrails soaked in dark, rich red
Marked the spot
Where the Pack finished its job.

No Geneva conventions apply in the natural world.
This Elk was 'lunch on the run' – fair prey.
What more can be said –
A hunter's missed opportunity – the Elk denied
The swift, lethal kindness of a bullet to the head.

We snow shoed to the half-eaten carcass – still fresh.
The Pack evidently had taken its fill.
Satiated but for how long?
Winter afternoons fade quickly in Northern Alberta:
We decide not to linger
In case they came back for dinner.

Lone Wolf

A lone wolf came by at twilight
While I sat on the bench beside the old garage.
Sixty pounds of misty grey –
Pointed ears,
Extended snout,
Large, splayed paws –
A Sheppard on steroids
Too pure to be a 'Coywolf'.

He paused briefly on the lawn freshly mowed
Taking no notice of my silent stare.
Gave himself a supple shake
And casually went his way
To the wooded gulch across the road.

Left me in another place –
Thoughts stretched:
There's water on Mars.

Balcony Thought: Edmonton Apartment

Alberta is rich

Robins in Ontario

Are fatter.

Balcony View: Edmonton Apartment

Dove and Magpie perched side by side

Atop a concrete car park.

I couldn't tell if they tweeted

But they seemed content.

Two birds of a different feather

Together – unruffled.

Hunger Games at the Moscow Zoo

The bears are melancholy; the gorillas are depressed.
They can't understand why their tasty Polish apples
Have suddenly been banned.

The giraffes miss their assorted vegetables
Imported from the Netherlands
Orangutans opine for Dutch peppers no longer available.

Cranes and Penguins are perturbed
About the lack of their preferred dish –
Baltic herring and South American fish.

And the Sea lions are absolutely flummoxed
Over the loss of their Norwegian crustaceans
That they so love to crack open.

The list went on for Moscow Zoo inhabitants
Who knew nothing of the Kremlin's bad behaviour,
Imposed Western sanctions and the 'tit for tat' exchanges.

Russian edibles which they sniffed and nudged with distain,
Did not appeal to their 'Westernized' palates.
It was like replacing Coca Cola with leftover Kvass.

The passive protest gave top officials pause.
Unlike humans, they could not be threatened,
Bribed, forced fed or simply sent off to Gulag exile.

Alas, the Zoo dwellers could not play the hunger games for long
Before the instinct for survival kicked in.
They'd soon eat what was given and bear it with a grin.

Incoming

I hear thunder distantly rolling
Baritone burbles edging closer.
The prelude to a thousand timpani
Assailed by mad Japanese drummers
Accompanied by an electrifying light show
Ending in torrential applause.

I stand inside the open garage door
Flick the Bic to my corona
In anticipation.

Part Two

Firefly – Ark

I stare at the night sky dragging on my corona.

Clouds dissipate; the stars sit bright.

Through the curling smoke I spy a faint flashing light

On and off; on and off – precise intervals

A steady bead across the horizontal curve.

Oddly, I thought of a firefly winking in the dark

Except this nocturnal beetle was a man-made ark

Encased with humans behind that abdominal glow

En route to – wherever they go.

When Stones Speak

(for Joan)

Water polished – glacier gouged
Granite hard – crystallized quartz
Onyx black – multicoloured hue …
Matters not which stones speak
Only that they do
To those with affinities to hear listen

Stones speak to the inner core
About place in the 'great chain of being'
Of broken links and the 'order of things'.

Stones speak amid rays of grainy light splayed
Nature playing with nurture
Each the other's nursemaid.

Sometimes stones speak intimately
Of loves and lovers, relatives and friends
Nebulous travellers in between
Framed imperfectly – memories frayed.

Stones speak of innocence lost,
Paths taken – others not,
Meanings once clear – now clouded.

Stones speak in mystical tones, allegorical whispers
Wrapped in divine wonders – mostly muted.

Stones speak sublimely – seldom unkind;

Thoughts clarify, trapped for a precious tranquil moment

Before emptied into the turbulence of time.

Stones do speak

To those with affinities to hear listen.

Go Train Distractions

Just before Rouge Hill station
As the clickety-clack of the westbound Go train slows
I cast a glance on a cold Lake Ontario
Shivering under a curtain of winter clouds sitting supreme –
Bulbous billows of corduroy grey blanketing the horizon.

A distant kingdom lay beyond this foreboding barrier I thought
Like Narnia or Middle Earth
Inhabited by assorted characters with chronicles to tell.

Imagine my surprise when suddenly a dragon emerged
Parting the misty shroud with practiced panache:
Golden wings – gracefully fluttering a fandango beat,
Attached to a scaled blue torso – lithe and serpentine,
Replete with orange spots judiciously placed down its corrugated length.
The emerald eyes blinked me a wink as if to say watch.
It hovered, with great flourish looped once
Then proceeded to a fanciful figure eight,
Took a bow and disappeared into the silvery ripples.

* * *

None of my fellow travellers saw the creature.
But why would they?
Those not adrift in sleepy haze were preoccupied
With their hand held devices
Peering intently into shiny screens
Finger flipping – exercising opposed thumbs.
Understandably, they were distracted

But, I hasten to add, not disconnected.
The world touched their fingertips.
And although they didn't notice the 'busking' dragon,
I'm sure that they found nestled in their palms
Equally wondrous things.

Thoughts during a Winter
Walk on Knox Mountain

Knox Mountain in winter –
An upheaval of ancient ash and lava
Thinly cloaked in a brownish verdant cover.
Ponderosa Pine, Douglas Fir and wild grasses
Pruned prosy.

We attack Knox's sullied banks
Taking a trail of moderate grade –
One of a dozen that carved loops into its grizzled flanks.
The earth crumbled loose under our well clad feet,
Each step sand paper gritty, estranged from the volcanic rock beneath.

Pleasantly flushed with exertion, legs fatigued,
We stop ascent midway at Crown Point look out.
To the south, Kelowna sprawls, sloshing against the valley sides,
Adjacent, Lake Okanagan curves its pinky finger northward,
A shimmering sheen against the sullen sky
In sharp relief to surrounding shallow soiled hills nearby
Like Knox, dressed in the same brownish verdant attire.

We nod, appreciating the panoramic view
And start the trek down – our quest complete.
Content to follow the main paved route
That runs from the bottom gate to the Pavilion at the peak.

Knox Mountain, civilized and urbane
Remade for sport and recreation.
Replete with official paths, wooden steps and railings
Leading to gazebos, kiosk benches and rest rooms at the top
Designed and detailed in a comprehensive plan of conservation
That tethered nature to a 'Park'.

Knox Mountain, 'preserved and protected'
To accommodate our hike and those of fellow travellers,
A laudable compromise and reasonable goal
That beckons causal walkers and outdoor revellers
While leaving the Mount – mostly whole.

Still, at times the wounded land must groan
As its carpet is worn thread bare.
And along its steep, buff grey cliffs
On some cold, mist shrouded day
When birds perch idle and humans huddle,
The Mount might say 'No more' and evoke a violent shiver
To shake – off the invading hordes
Like tawdry ticks into the lake
Letting the Kokanee Salmon
Pick at the bait.

Vanity

Cataracts removed,

The old woman stares into the mirror aghast.

"What have they done to my face!"

Vanity: 'Part Deux'

Not sure when it happened really –
Somewhere between the hair turning grey
And completely thinning.
I became invisible
To beautiful women!

Anti – Doped

Gave blood today
Went for a jog
Felt a mile too long
And a pint short.

Inscrutable Old Men

Inscrutable old men sit on creaking chairs
Smoking and/or having a brew
Peering out from open garage doors.

Flushed faces pinched in rumination
Blurry bits of lives lived and relived.
Triumphs, defeats, joys, sorrows,
Delusions and illusions mixed in between;
Vagaries long suppressed without redress are resurrected.

Reruns matter to inscrutable old men who linger in memory lane
Sitting on creaking chairs
Smoking and/or having a brew
Peering out from open garage doors.

'Timmy' Queens and 'Coffee Time' Kings

'Timmy' Queens and 'Coffee Time' Kings:
Retired, early morning risers.
Huddled over java cups and stir spoons
Prufrock's* neuroses no longer a theme –
Midlife crises subdued or forgotten,
No urge to dwell on thwarted desires
Or lament "what might have been":
All that's left behind as youthful indulgence.

The talk now is of travel – warm places to visit,
Getaways from the winter weather
And notes exchanged of a personal nature –
Offspring, grandkids – their wants and ambitions.
Ditto for ailments and medical conditions,
Usually kept light with smiles and positive spins.
Wayward politicians, overpaid sports stars and extravagant show biz types
Are also fair game around the table
And comic relief from the crossword puzzles in the complimentary paper.

'Timmy' Queens and 'Coffee Time' Kings:
Retired, early morning risers.

* Reference to J. Alfred Prufrock in T. S. Eliot's poem *The Love Song of J. Alfred Prufrock*

'Zoomer'

I used to be a senior – now I'm a 'zoomer'.
It sounds swankier and cuts a wider swath.

A 'zoomer' – 45 and older – is a former 'boomer'
Who by definition still has 'zip' –
Even if a bit of the bang has fizzled.

It's a marketing term; I have no illusions
Commercialized in mags and retirement home ads.
Old is the new young the message purports
"Embrace life" and go for the "absolute best" –
Do whatever needs doing on your bucket list.

Seems quite self-indulgent without much contrition –
Not an overly noble state of mind.
On the other hand, what better epitome of the human spirit
Than to 'zoom' the night away into that final light.

'Action Heroes'

What happened to my action heroes?

Arnold, Bruce and Sylvester,

You're suddenly senior citizens just like me!

No wonder your big screen moves lacklustre

And your framed figures seem puffy.

For years you've been commendable

Now you're quite expendable –

A fate that befalls inevitably.

But then you blow my old guy thoughts asunder

'Cause in Hollywood, you still lure leading ladies thirty-three and under.

House Ghosts

The new house has no ghosts; the old one had a few.
Although not always friendly, they were loath to start a fight.
They rarely caused great mischief; did not make loud noises;
No objects were sent flying or even set askew;
No portentous plots were hatched; and nothing went bump in the night.
At times, perhaps, they wanted to – some opportunities arose.
But the closets proved too shallow for deep despair or dander
No binding bonds were built with these spatial spooks and ghouls.
Thus, they did not come out to say goodbye.
Neither did we linger in case they changed their minds.

The new house has no ghosts; some, no doubt, will emerge.
Like us, they will be older, matured and vested,
Emptied of effusive embitterment and festering fears.
They'll appear in casual attire – wool knit sweaters and plaid shirts;
Becalmed and well rested, letting the past lay in peace –
Framed and hung in the morning sun with the best side showing.

Memory Stick

Every person deserves a memory stick
For life lived – short, long, fulfilled or wasted –
If not in whole, at least some meaningful fragments;
To be copied, shared and stored in a safe place
Just to say: "I passed by
Here's my imprint
However faint: however small."

Better that than graveyards and tombstones;
Cold containers for emptied souls
Marked by exiguous epitaphs.

Waitress Savvy

Never say to a waitress

"We're not quite ready to order,"

Or "Take your time with coffee and dessert –

I want to finish my drink."

Those are messages in code.

You'll wait for as long as it takes

A duck to come along

And kick you.

Troubled Souls

No matter how far away I go from here
On arrival, I find them there.
Troubled souls with woeful stories to tell.
Once started, they spill their guts like a broken water main;
The flow becomes relentless:
Distress, misdeeds, untimely deaths, loves lost or unrequited –
A catalogue of misfortunes selected and assorted
Compressed and unloaded without compunction –
Sad summaries of profound regrets and neglects.

I understand the need of letting demons out into the light –
A cathartic deliverance of sorts.
Still, I wonder at the zeal and zest of these verbal blogs –
Some best left for confessional pews, priests and rosary beads –
Until an old shrivelled lady with a work-worn face and enigmatic smile
Let it out of the bag.
"It's true," she said. "I've had my share of misery.
Experiences that left many bitter memories
But I wouldn't trade them now – not for a lifetime of greener grass somewhere else –
'Cause it's who I am; it's made me me.
Without my troubles I'd lose my way
And truly be unhappy."

Smile: A Sonnet

It is not the wantonly playful toss of hair
Coyly ruffled – black, blond or shades of brown;
Not the dimpled cheeks brushed rouge for added flare:
Nor the satin skin beneath the gown;
The heuristic hint of a secret scent;
The cleavage from the bra cups' tightened lift;
The well-shaped legs in yoga bent;
The petulant pose and flirtatious tilt;
The naked neck and sensuous lips;
Not even the whispered words over moonlight drinks
From a sultry tongue that sublimely slips
Suggestive thoughts with erotic links.
It is the inviting smile which sparks the eyes and ignites the glow
That lights the window to the soul.

Reservoir Walk

Don and I would take the Reservoir Walk
As often as we could in early afternoon –
A reprieve from the day's work routine.

We'd stroll out the College's south doors
To the carbon black ribbon of asphalt that curled
Around the man-made lake – sometimes slough.

Like the Walrus and the Carpenter*, we'd speak of many things
Mundanely of those profound
And quite profoundly on the most mundane.

From office politics to global events
With serendipitous gibber in between
There was much to consider and even more to explain.

We'd voice opinions, dole out wisdoms,
Fully feed our caustic wits and even
Solve long percolating problems that beset the human race.

At mid route we'd take an indulgent detour,
A small side trip to Tim Hortons –
Two medium regular – both to go.

It served testimony to our good form –
To walk, talk, drink coffee from a paper cup
And not dribble a single drop!

A heady time those Reservoir Walks,

A ritual I still remember fondly –

Now elevated to iconic status like a '57 Chevy.

*Lewis Carroll's poem in *Through the Looking-Glass* (1871)

Reservoir Walk 'Part Deux'

The recurring observations finally registered.
Like masked men entering a bank
The parade of casual callers could not be ignored.

The tiny bungalow with the unruly, overgrown yard
On a tucked away lane just a block from Timmy's
Attracted some decidedly dodgy dudes

Who with rapacious raps on the side porch door
Affected a crack wide enough to enter
Followed by quick, surreptitious exit.

"Not a brothel … must be a druggie depot," Don surmised.
His keen eye first spotted the suspicious suspects thus expanding
Our reservoir walk to include the 'stake-out' stroll.

Neighbourhood store offering pharmaceuticals for recreational use/abuse
Seemed a reasonable assumption –
Almost as wanton as the whorehouse scenario.

Confirmation of sorts arrived: a purple Impala cab
Slowly circled the block before rolling to a stop
A discreet distance beyond in the College Park lot.

Four stubby men with sketchy faces and sweaty clothes
Spilled out, then nervously dispersed
Only to re-emerge one by one at the door.

Transactions done, they slinked off, heads down,
Necks compressed, ball caps pulled over the eyes,
The telltale taxi suddenly sitting at the end of the street.

One day we spied no dudes or developing queues.
The bungalow appeared abandoned, empty with the dirty blinds gone.
A hint of disappointment hung; we enjoyed our nark patrols!

A small sign in the window beckoned us forward.
"Can you make it out?" Don asked
"An announcement – the print is too small," I responded.

"Maybe it moved – new business location?" Don wondered.
We kept squinting and striding until we got within range.
"Nope," I replied. "Nothing like that."
Curiosity, it is said, killed the cat
We were merely caught – in a mug shot
"Smile," the notice advised, "You are on camera."

Signed: RCMP

My Ride

Hop in Goldilocks
For a groovy ride
In my '78 Audi Fox.

It's robin egg blue –
A splash of colour from the '70s
That's still eye-catching cool.

Settle in: the seats are ergonomically correct
Velour/Vinyl over well-shaped foam
Perfectly tailored to your bum and back.

It has a '70s scent 'cause of the plastic and glue.
A sweet polyvinyl potpourri
That sets the mood.

Think strobe lights, miniskirts and high-heeled boots
Shags and sideburns, the Beatles
And your Elvis roots.

So hop in Goldilocks
'Cause I drive groovy
In my '78 Audi Fox.

The Meaning of Golf Balls

What's up with all these golf balls
That I keep finding
Buried in the garden,
Nestled in the grass,
Stuck inside the cedar hedge –
Titleist, Topflite, Molitar, Maxi Fli,
Galloway, Srixom and Royce.
Dulled by dirt, scuffed and scraped,
They simply appear when I dig or rake.

I pondered the mystery of these scattered spheres.
Surely bashing small, hard, dimpled globes
Was more than an inane act just to see
How far a Wilson Staff 4 flew off a battered tee.
There had to be more to it –
A deeper meaning exercised
Involving some cathartic release or titillation
That could explain this strange surprise.

I gave such musings a mulligan
To be used at a future date
While I put my assorted collection
In a grade 'A' egg carton crate
For delivery to my 'golfing' friend.
But then my curiosity was piqued again
When another oddity was served:
Among the rustic carrots and reddening tomatoes
A ghetto of green tennis balls arose.

Help Call to a Cellular Phone Company

Cell phone not working? Billing issues? Need tech help? Be advised: those friendly voices at the other end of your 800 number cannot help you. They're just there to empathize – to say: "I hear you" "Sorry about your trouble" and to give you another 800 number that the voice cheerfully assures can help you.

After a suitably interminable wait with a periodic recorded message (elevator music in the background) that affirms: "Your call is important to us", the other 800 number gets you a new pleasant voice from a different Department.

This voice can't help you either but she is profusely empathetic as well, obviously having taken the same company 'Customer Relations 101' course. She offers to provide another 800 number that would connect you to someone who might be able to help.

Don't bother. This connection is to an overseas voice and you wouldn't be able to understand it. Besides, no human at the other end of your call can, in fact, help you: it's a 'systems error' that will sort itself out … whenever.

Your aggravation, already acknowledged by numerous empathetic voices, may be somewhat mitigated by a token discount or rebate for your trouble. However, this occurs only after you have written a letter to the Better Business Bureau outlining your issue and remedy sought.

Part Three

Karate Kumite Haiku 1

Bow to most worthy foe.

Inner strength summoned, outer calm,

Eyes set in steely stare.

Karate Kumite Haiku 2

Focus – no distraction.

Relax amid the mounting tension.

Compose for combat.

Karate Kumite Haiku 3

Eyes first, then the feet.

Measured movement, the distance breached.

Sidestep, strike – hi yee!

tlhIngan may' jach

lel 1Ij batlh nuHvam

pep 0 jen qey1IS'Daq je Sto'vo'kor'Daq

DaHjajlu maj poH Heghqanq.

Klingon Battle Cry* (Haiku)

Clasp your honoured weapon

Raise it high to Kahless and Sto'vo'kor

Today is a good day to die!

*Klingon prose and English translation is based on Marc Okrand,

The Klingon Dictionary: English/Klingon, Klingon/English

(Pocket Books, New York, 1992). A great deal of 'poetic licence' was

taken with both the Klingon and the translation to English.

- Kahless: mythical warrior who unified the Klingons and became their first Emperor.
- Sto'vo'kor: where honoured Klingons go in the afterlife (Klingon equivalent of Heaven).

Big Bang

(A *Sheldon* **Thought)**

The big bang blew out debris bits shaping the celestials – solar systems, galaxies –

Sparkling, spiralling specks seemingly hung on an endless canvass of black.

Out there around countless remote suns orbit 'Goldilocks Planets' where life sparked.

Anomalies no doubt – like black pebbles on a white sand beach.

Still, there it is – we're proof and statistically far from unique!

The rest remains 'dark matter' spewing outward by 'dark energy' into the … empty.

Bad news! There is no pulling back – though gravity bravely tries.

The universe is on a one-way expansion into the cold, far flung … nothing.

This is no fugue thought or delusional rave.

Even string theory, bubble multiverse proponents concede it's true.

Our fate and that of at least a million other civilizations is sealed.

Some billion years forward all salient beings will exhale

One last whimper and wink out of existence.

Aliens with Golden Rules

They came from across the cosmos to save humans from themselves.
They never granted us an audience or deemed to explain why
But they did communicate concern and their deep disapproval
Of the way we treated each other in all parts of our world.
Thus, after much study, they decreed a set of golden rules.

Henceforth, we were to be magnanimous, kind and tolerant with all sentient beings.
We were to follow 'honest' truths and from what within we knew was just.
'Trojan' gifts were forbidden; fair play was now the new norm.
Weapons of mass destruction were null and void as were violent acts
No matter the merits of the cause or extreme the provocation.

The aliens made clear – the rules were firm with little room to fudge.
Those who sought to ignore them were told in diplomatic terms
Non-compliance was not an option – we could not obfuscate
Time was of the essence; there was an expiry date.

Of course, there were protesters, those who had much to lose.
Included were numerous dictators, junta generals and 'tin pot' tyrants.
Indignantly they denounced the imposition of this 'fascist' decree.
"We make the rules and decide how we're to govern," they decried
Defying the 'wanton' warnings while agitating citizens
Against these meddling aliens from the depths of outer space.

One by one they died quite unexpectedly in their beds.
Their time did indeed expire as that of their closest colleagues
Who also fell to the gentle wrath of unseen forces and 'passed on'.
Lesser associates were spared after announcing they had 'changed their ways'.
Thereafter, good and evil – assorted shades in between – merged
Into nebulous benevolence that was celestial if not divine.

Strange then, that after all the purging, strident critics reappeared
Wanting to abolish the golden rules (and rid the aliens who brought them).
They wrapped themselves in national flags, ethnic symbols
And in a show of chauvinistic pride, declared they preferred their own Caesars
To the ones inflicted from beyond – no matter the noble purpose or how kind.
Repression and despair, they asserted, are necessary for humanity to survive:
"For without pain and suffering we will have no gain."
"Ambition, competition and a nasty touch of malice is essential to our spirit,
It nurtures our creative genius that would be wrong to deny –
We must endure, struggle through our own shortcomings or wither away and die."

The puzzled aliens rejected such a premise and cauterized the message.
Promoters of this heresy were reprimanded – given atonement therapy.
Still, the critics persisted – in fact, multiplied.
A paradox of human nature – never quite understood –
Erasing 'bad behaviour' with 'live by' rules for common good
Only brings resentment and ingratitude.

The Dinosaur Song*

Let's go back into history
Where I will show and you will see
A ridin' along and along they ride
A mouchin' and a pouchin' and a licking their hide.
Here they come and a count them four
One, two, three and a dinosaur.
Well you see them big and you see them strong
And you see them as they mope along.
Now there's a cave man and he's hangin' around
And he's gonna hunt those dinosaurs down.
Cave man, cave man, watch your step
For when one comes you better get set.
Well the cave man didn't take what I said
And he went after the biggest fed.
Now the bones of the cave man shout
At the mean ole dino who stomped him out.
And now you know about a history
I think now that the cave man will see
A dinosaur's big and a dinosaur's strong
And you can't knock one to the ground.

*Children's song (music not included).

CPSIA information can be obtained at www.ICGtesting.com
Printed in the USA
LVOW07s0002120215

426668LV00001B/43/P

9 781460 262443